Dancing Alone

BkMk PRESS

University of Missouri-Kansas City

Sylvia Griffith Wheeler

POETRY

Dancing Alone

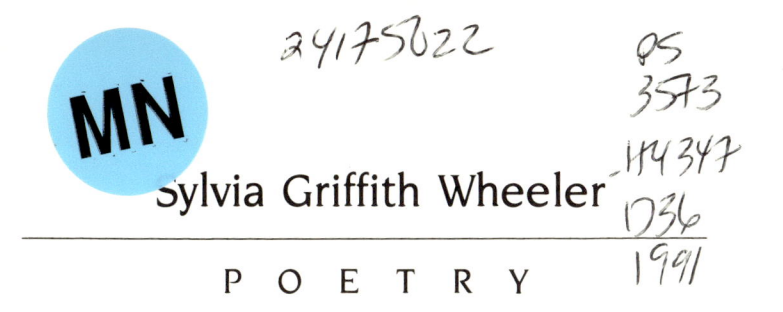

CREDITS

- "My Daughter/Her Boyfriend/My Poem," *City Limits* (BookMark Press, 1973).
- "After The Way," "Coyotes," "Early Morning Son," "Lost Contact," "Our Town Re-run," "Root Words," "Upwind," *This Can't Go On Forever*, (Raindust, 1978).
- "Wet Sunday," *Helicon Nine* (Vol. I No. I, 1979).
- "Hotel/Cafe poem," *Dacotah Territory* (No. 16, 1980).
- "Father Poem," *Dacotah Territory* (No. 17, 1980).
- "Vermont," *Long Pond Review* (No. 6, 1980).
- "A Woman Guards The Mona Lisa," *Northeast* (Number 21, 1981).
- "Taking Down Chagall's Blue Bull," *Chariton Review* (Vol. 8, No. I, 1982).
- "Another Barn Painting," *New Letters Reader* I (Univ. Missouri, Kansas City, 1983).
- "Higgins Beach: Gorham, Me.," "A New Fable of Taos Mountain," "Life: Sailor at Picnic," *Gryphon* (Vol. 10, Issue 1, 1984).
- "Waving To Farmers," "The Prairie Cafe," *Great River Review* (Vol. 6, No. 2, 1985).
- "Square," *In The Middle* (BkMk: Univ. of Mo., Kansas City, 1986).
- "Mother In The Rock Shop," *Clockwatch Review*, (Spring, 1991).

Thanks to The MacDowell Colony and The South Dakota Arts Council for affording me time to work on this manuscript.

Poems Copyright © 1991 by Sylvia Griffith Wheeler

Typography, Book Design: Michael Annis

Library of Congress Cataloging-in-Publication Data
Wheeler, Sylvia Griffith.
  Dancing alone : poems / by Sylvia Griffith Wheeler.
   p.   cm.
  ISBN 0-933532-81-4 : $7.50 paper
  I. Title
PS3573.H4347D3   1991
  811'.54—dc20   91-2611
                                                                             CIP

Financial assistance for this book has been provided by the Missouri Arts Council, a state agency.

BkMk Press brings readers the best in contemporary American poetry and international literature. A small literary press, unique among university publishers, Bk Mk ("Bookmark") Press operates under the aegis of the College of Arts and Sciences at the University of Missouri-Kansas City.

BkMk Press

Dan Jaffe, Director
Rae Furnish, Associate Editor

For My Sister Maria

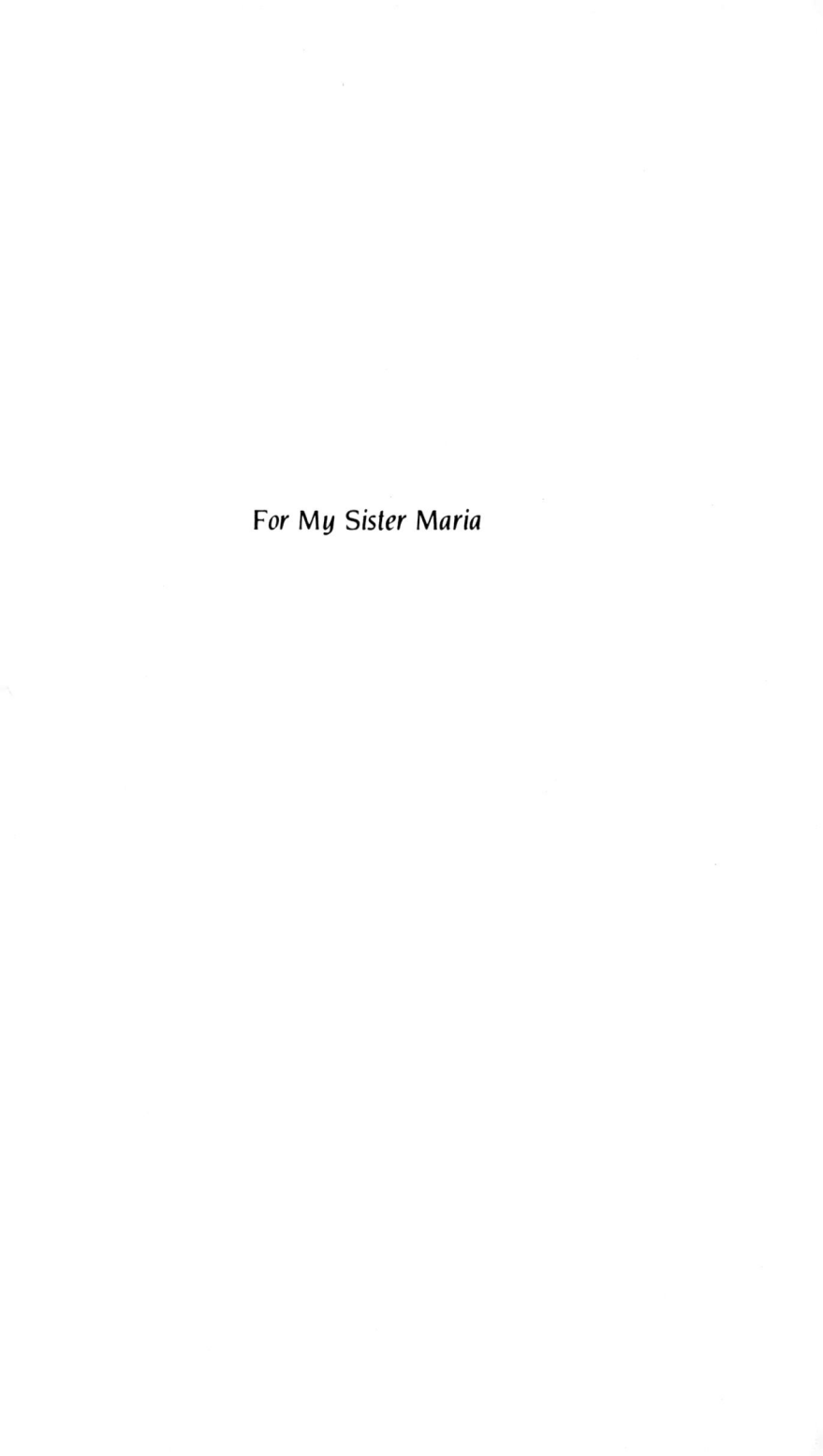

Dancing Alone

Square	8
Root Words	9
The Barking Dog	10
Train: Whistling back the '30s	12
Generations of Women	13
Huddle: Mother at 87	14
September 3rd	14
Life: "Sailor at a Picnic, Baylor County, VA, 1943"	15
Another Jane Poem	16
A Dream of Grandmothers	17
Our Town Rerun	18
After the Way	19
My Daughter/Her Boyfriend/My Poem	20
Another Barn Painting	21
August Letter	22
You Are Dying	23
Father	24
Taking Down Chagall's *Bull*	25
Divorce	26
The Old Exit Scene	27
Wet Sunday	28
Black and White	29
From the Aquarium	30

A Woman Guards the *Mona Lisa*	31
Quiet	32
Trestles	33
February	33
If You Would Lie	34
Notes from a Sea Cabin	35
Memorizing Touch	36
Grandmother's Feather Pillow	37
Hotels and Cafes	38
Waving to Farmers	39
Street Exchange	40
Falling Asleep on the Couch	41
The Slightest Wing Spread: 9 Stanzas	42
Vermont	51
New Hampshire Woods	52
Higgins Beach: Kennebunkport, ME	53
Chigger	54
Prairie Cafe	56
In this Photo Transparency	57
Now that the Bird Is Gone	58
Hurricane	59
Mother in the Rock Shop	60
Grand Lake, Grove, OK	61
Dancing on Sand	62
Like Croats	65
My Last Mistress	66
Stubble	67

Square

I walk by a square kind of house
with a square dry closed-in front porch
where kids in small midwestern towns
go slowly after school or on Saturday mornings
to take piano lessons in rooms
where tulip petals smudge dark tables
and the woman who boiled last night's
turnips stiffens on the bench.

Betty Lou Sullivan's peony white arms
fall over the keys June in tune
while some of us count out loud
back up and start over again.

Root Words

She shucked words
pocked from clean
rough from smooth
tainted from pure

She knifed dirt from sills
off shelves
out of cracks
into pails
under lids

She shined floors
brushed hair
bleached clothes
washed mouths
poked slouched spines

Remembering dust on the tongue
tracks through the sugar
she blanketed beds
curtained windows
weatherstripped the door
against wayward siftings

The Barking Dog

My dad's mouth was shaped like an "O." His ears stuck out. I don't know how death ever got him. He thought he'd live forever, that he'd fool death by falling asleep, pretending not to hear, or simply ask, "Sir?" in that way of his and death would see the error.

I was nine when he came back from New York with the dog. Still wearing his black worsted coat and his hat, bag and briefcase in hand, he sat down on the floor to show us how the dog barked. He was at one end of the room and Maria and I at the other waiting. First Dad lined the dog up, centering him on the carpet, checking the little rubber bulb you squeezed to jump dog along, then petting the dog's fuzz, he told us about seeing Tallulah Bankhead co-starring with Donald someone in Blythe Spirit. He'd seen it on Broadway and after the show he'd bought the dog. Dad was interested in Donald because he'd come to Dad's college in 1928 as a visiting actor, and Dad had acted alongside him in The Importance of Being Earnest.

Dad gave the bulb a squeeze and Scottie jumped like he

knew he was in Kansas. Dad said of all the dogs the peddler was selling, this one had caught his eye because when he'd bent down to look at it, it barked its head off. Dad shook his head thinking about it. It was amazing how those dogs barked.

With the second squeeze Scottie fell over, and Dad righted him, rubbing his fur. The dog was three or four inches long, made of tin, and covered with black cotton hair. Dad squeezed and Scottie leapt forward an inch. Now he had the rhythm, and the two of them, Dad and dog, moved down the room toward us. As they came nearer, Dad stretched out behind the dog so Scottie could come to us unaided by the human hand. We were to send him back. But when he came close enough to touch, I knew I'd seen better dogs before, and they didn't bark either.

Other Sunday afternoons Dad got tangled up in the water sprinkler hose and Maria and I had to get him out. We'd pull at the green hose like frenzied firemen. Dad needed our full help. He would quickly fall exhausted into the wooden lawn chair and continue to instruct us to make a tight circle of the hose. Sunday evening we would walk to the picture show. When he was a boy, Dad had seen every silent film made. Now he couldn't wait to see Jimmy Stewart or Betty Grable or Betty Hutton. When he was dying I told him he'd done everything he could hope to do. He said, "No," he'd wanted to be an actor.

Train: Whistling back the '30s

Tonight I love the whistle
its polite toot
sent down the line

Who does it tell what to
other than the hills
other than the family eating waffles
in the yellow kitchen beside the tracks

Ma Pa Buster
Pearlie and Sonny
whistling Home Home Home

Generations of Women

Generations of women have looked out windows
at first snow the smell of soap
and grease behind them zwieback
from small mouths wetting their shoulders

They have told stories
of porridge waiting in bowls
of brothers disguised as swans
of Rose Red and the sigh of her
comb in the fur of the brown bear

Thinking themselves disguised as arms
breasts laps with little cause to think
they've pushed their names through window frost
wondering if laprobes in Russian sleighs think
or Alpine meadows absorbing thaw think
or cloths covering tables

Huddle: Mother at 87

Mother, if we huddle,
can I keep you from
the Boogie Man. Does he
mistake you for age —
your giggle, your open eyes?

Does he take our huddle
for a bow? Then, stand up,
pretend to be what you are,
you who have meant no harm.

September 3rd

Even the hills sleep in this fallow
season   Spread and content they sleep
alone   The corn sleeps   Just the youngest
of dry stalks yawn in the breeze   Grass
under the dew's too heavy to lift its head
The windmill half a barn are dead   Even
the dead move sometimes in the wind

Life: "Sailor at a Picnic, Baylor County, VA, 1943"

This blond face beneath the sailor cap,
this 1940s mouth kissing the soft sky,
the arc of watermelon seed.
These fingers smooth enough to touch
without touching the glossy page,
knuckle lines just forming, pudgy
the way we're pudgy into our late teens.

Suppose warriors had first to draw the body,
the shared edge of flesh and sky,
the fullness of mouth and groin,
the muscle flowering in a lifted arm,
butterfly wings of rib cage.

Suppose a pencil felt these lines,
rib by rib, by curve,
would it be so easy?

Another Jane Poem

"What time is it?" we'd ask the old
woman curled in the door of her old
house   We were nine and knocked at age
What relief to find ourselves whole
when she shut us out

I write this to you Jane
as we begin that curling in

Think of the cathedral clock
where the wooden family comes out to bow
the child the youth the parent grandparent

The longest bow belongs to childhood
doesn't it?

Would you ask them in Jane
if they knocked?
Nor did she shuffling
from our eyes fixed on her lace curtain

A Dream of Grandmothers

Last night, I forded old roads.
All but the cemetery's were washed out.
Saw you, stiff-legged,
come as fast as a cane can
to open my car door.
Heard your summer voice.

Waking, I had no one
to tell, and was afraid of forgetting.
And if I could tell
afraid they'd put it wrong—
set up Old Dodge, 1930s,
turn on the wind machine.

Our Town Rerun

Miz Dr. Gibbs, Mr. Constable,
Miz Gossip and Mr. Town Drunk
sitting on their heavenly chairs
waiting for the eternal to come out,
then Miz Emily, dead in childbirth,
comes up, wants, as they do not,
the brief return to earth,
to catch once more Mother's eye as she
walks between range and kitchen table,
Father's smile behind the evening news,
the sound of little brother's high-pitched voice
(before he goes from a burst appendix at Scout camp)
to pass again down Main Street, say hello
to the friendly druggist squirting seltzer
in cherry phosphate and back
by the old school house, remembering graduation white,
and home to the linked hands around the table,
and the alfalfa sweet smell of spring fields,
the train whistling through the night,
and a sun warmed cheek against your cheek
and food and sleep and morning.

And I am crying, crying, in the dark,
can't see the little screen, only hear
voices, young and old, and train whistles,
and silverware ringing the plate and wind through the old elm,
telling myself, Thornton Wilder's a sentimentalist,
Thornton Wilder's a sentimentalist, Thornton Wilder's a
    sentimentalist.

After the Way

we broke this land
taking blade to seed
trampling paths
the hedgerow sheared
timothy checked

that a hook-beaked
rough legged
hawk
should post
its spotted silk
on the porch rail
that our eyes should meet

My Daughter, Her Boyfriend, My Poem

She writes
what she says
is not a poem,
is, instead,
about a poem
where he called
her a road
he wanted
to explore,
telling her
of girl roads
he'd cycled down before.

She tucks
thin books
of wise sayings
next to her compact;
from her window,
mountain mist's
sad like tears.
She knows, wants
me to know she knows,
alleyways
from country roads.

All this I've heard.
And anyone

who calls life
a road,
or thinks rain's
like tears
has a long way to go.
But, it's his cycle,
her window,
my poem.

Another Barn Painting

Eyes dulled
they paint the barn
pig color

pink through mud crusts
Clay
seeping out banks
Kaffir
Tassel bead dust
or gravel down roads
River birch buds
Fungus curling off old wood

August Letter

I'm water in a slow pond.
Algae holds the air.
You'd like it here—
time, trees, a chair in the shade.
Old turtle under the porch
sticks his neck out each June,
then sits down.
Blood ambles to the brain.
I could stretch back,
grow old like this.
You'd say, Look at that turtle
in the lawn chair—Look
at that wrinkled mud
where the pond's died.

You Are Dying

and grape leaves, thin as papyrus,
lucid as skin on bone,
deny their purple property.
No color, tendrils snap.

In wet air,
leaves, big as emblems,
chamois soft,
shake easy from the wood.

Some, from winter buds,
seed hard, fall
pale into the creek.

Others, on the vine,
hold the day.

Father

To see the body change,
feet pink clean of wear,
jowls to bone.

I try to think you looked like this,
pink and bone at 12, 14,
but the eyes are too hot,
and your arms won't work.

I act as the nerve
positioning them to comfort
as they positioned me, young.

It is the neck,
knobbed and chorded,
holding your head like a question mark.

When your father died you didn't look at him,
not wanting that memory
and you ask us not to linger.
But I stare,
needing to know how it's done.

Taking Down Chagall's Blue Bull

It is the stuffed animal
standing at the foot of our bed — big blue
bloated   Broadside his unfocused eye
the bell at his neck

He has drunk all the blue from the water
under the triple arched bridge and the sky
I know because I have dusted him
as I have aired the pillows their faded
blue ticking

If I were a child
I would join the yellow women bouffant
crossing to the cottage in the foreground
We would open the door to smell cabbage
or soup to rest easy behind stucco
brush strokes

But it is the bull I see

If I were a child
I wouldn't take any of this seriously
That a bull standing beside a blue
vase of flowers three times larger
than the little man could be broad and deep
and cold as a river would be a
matter of fact

Divorce

Knowing there'll be no answer
I call the house hoping its innocence
is at home that it thinks itself lucky
or above the law

I ring the central staircase
calling back our comings up or down
to where we wanted or had to go

I call the bedrooms
the child who liked sunrise
the child who liked sunset
the child who kept his blinds pulled

I ask the walnut veneer of the family room
if the hundred penny nails pounded in
by a son's hand want out? And the field
whose limestone we plucked for a hearth
its stone back?

What of my shoe mud sucked off ten years
ago as we lay tile downhill? Does it float
or hold like a cornerstone?

And our secret places? Even
now as the next family steps sure
on floorboards sighing
"So long So long"

The Old Exit Scene

Everything is as it was,
shoes off the varnished floor,
desks clean of words,
dressers of bottles, brushes,
the beds stripped.

We are as we were
both of us wearing the clothes
we came in.

It is the old exit scene —
two people standing at the door
holding suitcases.

Another curtain down.
We are the ones who came
to the same place at the same time.

To exit we have these choices:
the lipsticked farewell,
the casual embrace,
the turn in opposite directions.

But not the words,
they've been taken away.

Wet Sunday

We could make clear distinctions
between words, or turn on some other noise.

We could cross our legs
and try to figure each other out.

We could remember eccentrics—
the girl who wanted to be a chicken when she grew up,
the parents who saved her.
The boy who wanted to be a car
and became one. Even out of gas he never walked.

We could drive off prairie sections
and say, "Look here."

We could fall through the attic of an old house
and read farm ledgers on moldy mattresses.

We could be elderberry wine beetles
wambling tree to tree
then take off our shells
to look at skin that never sees sun.

We could be something rain falls on somewhere else:
a Pacific peninsula
a Vermont maple
gray shingles
a Puerto Rican fern

or something rain falls on here.

Black and White

Your 1930 engagement photo
came in the mail
as if you let loose old images.
There is no letter.

I touch your face —
where pearls pulse your neck is warm.
Your eyes take a glow,
their familiar moistness.

The soft slope of shoulder.
Oh, I can see your body
tan as the underskin of birch
rise from the bath.

And the chin's lift.
What you wanted
and took care to keep.
Here your straight hair is marcelled,
the lightest waves.
You are young.

But I don't look long.

I put you back in the envelope
you came in,
handcanceled,
through the mail.

You see, Mother, I have a drawer for everything.

From the Aquarium

It's always raining in here
Outside Georgia pines brush soft as willow

We are so present
continents drift about us

I lean toward you
leaning toward fern

We rub scales in a fishy way
to see the night through

In this wave lift
our eyes are always open.

A *Woman Guards the* Mona Lisa

The woman guarding The Mona Lisa doesn't smile;
it's hot in here and her girdle rides the ridge,
nor do olive trees draw cool water to fruit.
There's no breeze.
She doubts Mona smiles at all,
and even if she was highborn (she also doubts this)
there's always supper to get on,
the burly boy to nurse.

The guard knows that look when she sees it.
One way or the other the woman was paid.
She flips a wrist at two boys leaning on the ropes.
"Back Off," she says. She'd like to slap them.
"S'il vous plait," she adds.
Her feet hurt. She'd give all the Italians in the room
for an afternoon off.

And she knows the patronizing act of a "good girl,"
how to hold quiet, impassive,
how to keep the shoulders back,
how to think of other things.
She looks for a bead of sweat painted over on Mona's neck.

The mountains were drawn in later—
the guard knows that—it was the convention.
And probably the mother-in-law lived with her.
No greens for supper, the pouting Maman,
the husband who rode her like a donkey.
That's why the eyelids fell. She was tired.
Tonight she'd say the bleeding was coming on,

but, mornings, she'd pull the bodice low,
look for another sitting.

When the guard goes home, she shuts the door,
takes the bed. She pulls her girdle off
and, carefully, the feet from her shoes.
Her lids drop, her lips loosen.
She almost smiles.
The job's been hers ten years now. She intends to keep it

Quiet

While I look at my crossed palm
you take your black walk

Yet you are young
disguised in argyle socks
and I can't dream

Nights we lean against walls
watching shoes dance
sure there are secrets
we don't understand

None who should know does
and haven't we said it?
Or we sit in coffee shops
raising our hands to the constant draft
lifting soup to our mouths

Trestles

The best poems I've read this year come from Kansas.
They are about people and quiet and rabbits.
They name rivers riding under trestles
where the Watkins boy hung by his fingertips
when the train passed and lived
or maybe his fingers were cut off and he fell
down to the brown and green walnut stain,
those long Kansas legs hanging there under the trestle.

February

It is the day a fox
will print grass stains on
December snow-shoed weavings
around my house. His ice
tipped ears will brush
dry on the shingles
— fox hair and deer hair
caught in the cedar.

These long trees lean
hairless over the roof.

If You Would Lie

This longing threatens my Sundays.
It is a parasite
with no head
to put tweezers to.

It is that queasy dangling
no music cures
nor hard labor
nor friend's need

A disease
of the young
and I have survived —
see the ripples on my stomach.

Where is the cowl
to keep my head straight?
my eyes?

If you would lie
beside me
just lie down
only the legs touching.

Notes from a Sea Cabin

1.
Carried back a starfish,
soft shapeless on my arm,
its seahole waning with the tide.
Put it on the porch.

2.
Cleaned the cabin—
put the candle on the defunct fridge,
weeds in a can on the one burner stove,
a picture of a chair and book on the wall.

3.
Brought up another star,
ten carmine arms,
put it between the jelly fish
and the pressed black sand case
a moon snail lived in.

4.
Cleaned the cabin—
set the musty mattress to air,
counted apples in the fridge,
arranged pencils in a jar.

5.
Caught a gull just in
from *The New Yorker*.
It keens and grooms
keens and grooms.

Memorizing Touch

In your arms
I curl upon
myself burrow
in the hollow
of your shoulder
breathing back
my breath and
yours   Intent
I suck my mouth
onto your summer
skin not wanting
to think you'd slide
me off into air   Now
deeper to the fur
of underarm
memory's dark and
musky way

Grandmother's Feather Pillow

I sit on an apartment deck
pluck quills from the ticking—
a puff of barnyard, a billow of Kansas.

White sheets over lines swell
like tents. Chickens scratch dust.
Girls come from under the tents
balancing buckets of water,
and there's no music except clover
and sheet's slap and chickens.

Tonight my head will roll
in the sun of it, in the softness
of your upper arms, in
the air, dust, water.

Hotels and Cafes
— for Ann

This time it's the hunter's rags and a polyethylene
duck held on the lap—
the two of us sitting as if we always sat
on the porch of Wakonda Hotel
waiting for Saturday morning.

Self-consciously silly, we wait
for you to make sense of it.
Photographer's models are like that,
tilting their heads as told.
Some Saturdays are like that too.

It is a fair full day in Wakonda
as it was in Alcester where we tilted
smiling out of a 1940 truck cab, 40 years
of old parts on the hood. In Elk Point
Dan took the park bench and I rose
from a city garbage can sipping walnut wine.
Taken in a good light, you can make sense
of Saturdays.

Unloading tripod, camera, costumes, selves
to the streets of South Dakota towns
causes you to assume Hollywood names.
I take "Cecily," Dan, "Hunk" and we give "Estrillida"
to the photographer who frowns
and says "Sioux Falls" when someone asks.
Saturdays are for buying groceries.

Following all this we stop at cafes
the E&I in Wakonda
(Half-cooked delburgers)
The Corner Cafe in Alcester
(with fries)
the Truck Stop outside Elk Point
(4 pickles each)
and then we go home to finish Saturday.

Waving to Farmers

Two in the summer field
stand in the beans to talk.
Winter, they talk at the Prairie
Cafe.   Spring, from a deep brown field.
Farmers' sons remember heads, legs,
haunches, rabbits, sometimes a cat,
fingers cut off in the blades,
a necessary loss.

Two pass in a truck,
rifle behind their heads.
I wave.   They wave back
even though I'm a woman
whose dark hair might be Indian.

Street Exchange

We were standing on the street.
You said I'm *depressed*.
What had that to do
with the easy exchange between strangers?

I tried chatter and gesture,
but the word's weight pressed against my hand.

I took it home and lay with it,
silence, the body's going, the mind's
circled me like well stones.

I tried to rise above it,
reached for fruit, book, friend,
but each was tasteless.
The sour mouth had become mine.

I wanted to find you,
hear you say it again,
not the symptom this time
but the word itself.

I thought if the street could hear it,
could see it cream and congeal on our lips,
I'd take it as tender of the real world.

Falling Asleep on the Couch

The three kids belonging to
the woman with three stomachs, #9A,
are taking naps.

A flock of bicycles rides through leaves.

I am at church camp
walking downhill with Norman Vincent Peale;
he tells me the word's a sure thing.

#9B puts on a little naptime music.

Next to the rose chintz chaise lounge
in my mother's house
a white phone rings softly.

The Slightest Wing Spread: 9 Stanzas

1.
I was the one under the juniper
who shrugged off loneliness
and under the dogwood
boredom respecting neither.
Now it is summer
and my friends are in danger.
They will find me in their beds,
bending their arms
to fit my shoulders,
turning their fingers
down on mine.

2.
Mother, you say
he returns in dreams—
you are dancing alone
when someone taps you on the shoulder,
says *Pretty Lady may I escort you
home?* You turn around.
It's Dad's tilted smile.

Or you're pushing a grey baby buggy
down silent streets of the '30s,
and he taps you on the shoulder.

Ah!

A tap on the shoulder.

3.
The student takes a pillow.
I cover his face with Mandelstam's bee stings.
He neither resists nor returns.
It is this innocence I like
the warm red rise of each cell.

My neighbor the lawyer crawls in.
She says in common law
intuitive response counts.
Jurors can enter
the changing color in a defendant's face,
the foot's inward turn.

My best friend gives me her hand
Like a child's spade,
a small v,
No, she says, *it's sensual.*

Perhaps, I say, *but more like a porcelain*
handled silver cake server.
The more I insist, the smaller it gets.

The one who would love me
is just out of reach.
He says, *If I'm going to sleep*
with you, lie still and be a quiet.

4.

You call us Fallen Angels
after those who could touch
three times a year.
But even that is denied us,
Airy one, for you
cannot love women.

You say there is no unearthly
reason for lips,
though pelvis and shoulder
blades please.

We close our eyes,
circle each other,
avoid the line of body to body.

My slightest wing spread
feathers your cheek,
turns your silky hair to down.

I carry it
home — wind against the web.

5.
A hair falls from my head
to your mouth.
This is what time puts between us.
Your fingers curl as if to pluck out a mint.
My fingers curl.
Your wrist snaps.
Mine.
There is passion in this.

6.
When I leapt from the bathroom to your bed
no moral perogative
nor artistic imperative
prevailed —
you can see by the language
they'd get in the way.

Forgetting it was your bed,
that it was my body
spread in the dark,
like childish fingers
over the keys,

I leapt,

hoping your eyes were open
to my audacity.

What?
you said,
no wonder, no surprise.

7.
And then we were Hepburn and Fonda,
time coming down on us.

We were Whitman's he-bird, she-bird
calling, *Here I am* to a wing in a glade.

No, we were both Hepburn,
just the bones left,
and in that hollow
we whispered of cottages and golden ponds,
neither of which we really cared about.

Awake, we were ashamed of bad lines,
borrowed drama,
sweet promising we hadn't earned
or said we wanted.

8.
You are
an eye
expecting space

A lean bone
with no expectations

I am space

You are
an eye
a lean bone
a leg twitch

We lie together
skull on skull

9.
Because we can't give each other
any lasting thing,
we roll like children
over and over in the bank's silt
until our skins are like shells.

The river will take anything
along the way, but we
hold each other lightly.

See what it does to the stones?

Vermont

The wooden chairs knee to knee
on the great lawn—

Imagine dreaming the lawn first
and then the summer house
as if there were all of time.

At the net a white
ball floats home.

And from the green lawn chairs,
talk moves into dark mountains.

New Hampshire Woods

Some of us seem meant to attend,
to rain on fern and forest lily
waving its deep blue seeds to
an impulse of air, to listen with
all ear to the worm wrinkling ground
or the mayfly's float leaf to leaf.

June's young branches let go
in and around gray trees, nuzzle
the mushroom fat and moist on
the cedar floor whose bed becomes
our bed, whose saplings our promise,
and so we stay thinking our arms lean
and loose as the vines they hang from.

Higgins Beach:
Kennebunkport, ME

When we rise to walk the beach
half in half out of water, harmless
protrusions please our bodies:
breasts cocks butts.

Waves shells wings fins
also curve for our pleasure,
our heads above the slick
smell of kelp, our feet
firm in sliding sand.

Children run from the sun
into cold water, their mouths
open, their arms rising
and falling like cilia.

A young couple waltzes
into the tide. Breakers
reach for their chests,
their pointed arms.

The old man hesitates,
lifts his arms high.
Three times he enters,
shakes himself, turns away.

Chigger

Mother was Kansas State's beauty queen, 1935, and is still vain. But she doesn't value vanity, she values mind. She wanted me to grow up "interesting." "Interesting" is my most frequently used word.

When Mother and I are together we're in some sort of contest. She reads and keeps up on what's going on in the world while holding fast to certain moral principles her reading only helps secure.

But she's not grim. At Christmas my sister gave her a life-sized battery run rat that shuddered across the floor in that slant-sided sneaky way. I couldn't stand to look at it. Mother sat there, squeezing the control and purring with pleasure as its velvet self sidled up my ankle.

"What," Mother asked me the last time we were together, "is the most amazing thing in the world?" I knew my answer had better be good, having to do with "Imagination," "Strength of character," "Square tomatoes." I said some of these things.

"No," she said, delighted I had failed. "The chigger."

"The chigger!" I said. This time she had done it, rising above all Midwestern credos to something truly quixotic. I knew I could never be so inventive, so interesting.

"The chigger," she continued, "has a heart."

"A heart? I doubt it," I said. "Probably some wire-like vein pulsing."

"No," she said. "A heart. Heart-shaped."

"Do you think a chigger has a brain," I said.

She didn't seem to care.

"My respect for the chigger is greater now," she said. "It's hard to scratch when you think of that little heart beating beneath your skin."

"But the brain is what tells the heart what to feel," I said. "So does the chigger have a brain?"

Mother was dropping the hem on one of my skirts while she told me this, and she clamped her teeth down on a couple of pins, pursing her mouth so the lines themselves looked like straight pins.

Prairie Cafe

Here's no sea, no unfamiliar habit or color.
The maroon plastic booth has split seats.
You know the smell of oil cloth;
because it's still summer, you move your hands
in front of your face to keep flies from landing.
Yours is the waitress who lived in the third floor room
in the old house on Pine St., the one
whose mattress caught fire last Sunday night
and burned the place down;
when you ask for two checks, her lips curl.
In the booth across sits the woman, barely in her halter top,
who is always stoned, and is again.
You know all this.
The lazy professor's pretty wife, her white teeth when she sees you,
the slightly tainted smell from the chicken as you turn your nose.
You look into the kitchen. Something spins under the sink.
You sit a long time because it's hot and muggy outside.
You keep your hands moving and pretend to have a good talk.
Sometimes your friend asks you to repeat yourself
and you know you're talking.

In this Photo Transparency

— for Cecelia

I am that dark spot
the squint eye sees

You put me back in your locket
face to face with others
picked up traveling
reduced to fit the gold
circle at your neck

In your breathing
we become family
kept in the dark from fading
Like family what we know
of each other is myth
lifted by you to this light
to that.

Now that the Bird is Gone

light can hang
in the corner
where he hung angry
and plants can perch
like cats on quiet
stools, their fur lifted
by air we almost hear.
Fire can drop burnt
edges to the grate,
and in the sigh
of fish we rest
our hands while
from the bedroom comes
the smell of sleep. I
feel your skin, each hair
in each cell rise,
as we climb the stair.

Hurricane

— for Pat

When we rode the Hurricane
I slid into your bones.
Twice you wanted out
but I set the bar
as if to call you coward
and locked it.

"Why can't I say no?" you asked.

I grow arrogant with age, a Ringmeister.

The idea behind the thing
is that you're thrown around
then dropped. Your head
met my shoulder, you closed
your eyes, said, "No"
to each fall.

I kept talking.

"It's better with your eyes open.
Look straight ahead."

Your mouth wet my neck.
I didn't look.

The last few turns were gentle,
"Like a chute opening," I said.
"Our feet nearly touch down."
It was that I'd refused —
the earth's quake beneath you.

Mother in the Rock Shop

Your hands dredge the trays,
lifting azurite, the obsidian
chip, a pink quartz and two
razored combs of coral. Finally,
you take a green and white
agate like the ocean outside.

I take the flat gray one,
the color of your hair,
your face, the color of my hair
my face. No one hinders us.

I remember
your anger, forty
years ago. You rowed away
from family breakfast to the shore
opposite our vacation cabin
leaving us behind
in the scrape of oar against stone.

Grand Lake, Grove, OK

Struck-dumb Bill
and his wife Marian
the garment worker
sit in their shored boat
waiting for Manet
their straw hats banded in paisley
blue tassels swinging from the brims

Bill lifts his glasses
on their neck string
to look around the dry
grass the boat sits in
toward the heavy water beyond
his blue tassels swinging

Dancing on Sand

I hold you in that cell
memory's marked did you wait
not for me and not for
morning and not in my house
but on another bed
in a room I've seen once.

It's hot you're in the maroon
bikini shorts one hand holds
Applause the other yourself
You look up   Alongside the drawn
shade's an oblong bar of moon
You think it's an academy award
You think of Warren Beatty's hips
You reach for *Real Sangria*

down half a bottle

When you come to my bed
I'm near sleep   You touch
my shoulder tell me
I've been good to you
then we're both gone
The bedsheets are not cool
or restless   They have fallen
on each other and smothered
the least flake

Today on sand
we shadow dance
my shoulder front yours back
my foot advancing   yours retreating
my palm forward yours away

More the measure of a cello
than a flute

When I feint
to your thigh
you stop

Further apart we resume

Your shoulder front mine back
your foot advancing mine retreating
your palm forward mine away
This time I try a knee

Your head shakes N*o*
The fog comes in

You must have a cell
marked by me   Tell me
what do I do there?

Like Croats

We danced a large slow circle
and faster doubled the circle shuffling
music with our feet stamping the music
to the floor. Ann said *Hold little fingers*
Paul said *Only an Arab would say that*,
so we danced snaking to the porch
tightening the loop till face to face
we couldn't turn back. We were not good
dancers but the jugged beer
danced brown on the table and the pink pale
and yellow Chinese crispies danced
and coconut rum danced in hands circling
the circling dancers. I said *Throw money*
Paul said *Only a Croat from Strawberry Hill
would say that* and we leaned 1 2 3 in and
kicked while the Welsh poet kissed Joanie
and Ted put his hand on Mary Jane
and we danced and Dorothy with her
cancer danced Paul said *Only Dorothy
could dance like that* and snow boots
on the front porch danced and, mellow
in the middle, Maithri from Sri Lanka danced

My Last Mistress

This is my mistress' arm. How fair. She used
to touch me here. And there — once a matched pair —
is her pectoralis. There, some hair. And,
ah, the legs, rectus, vastus, quadriceps
femoris, to the ankles she'd lock
about my spine, at the coccyx, to be
exact. Her foot. Her ear. Her hair was brown
and thick and hid my hand. The masseter.
Her teeth, she smoked, carbon markings of her
time. Rolled front, her eyes, exophthalmic,
were grey. The ancients thought the heart to be
symmetrical, time circled it, of all
the mummy's viscera was left intact.
Now, if you'll take that, we'll move beyond.
Serratis anterior; external
oblique. She complained. A weakness in the
feminine. The sartorius, longest,
"tailor's" muscle, let her double cross her
legs. She liked to sit in judgement until
I'd touch the abdominis and what
follows from it. And now we're back where
we began her. My mistress. Scan her.

Stubble

Desk clean   paper ready
the full morning light on
yesterday's words

Sun on snow stubble and trees
No footprints on the day
A shake of white against the blue pane

But I turn to the desk
hold yesterday to it
insist it come round,
kiss me with its truth.

SYLVIA GRIFFITH WHEELER's book *Counting Back: Voices of the Lakota and Pioneer Settlers* will be published by BkMk Press with the help of a grant from the Witter Bynner Foundation. Her other books include *City Limits*, poems; *In the Middle: Midwestern Women Poets*, anthology; and *For Kids, By Kids*, anthology. Her play, *This Fool History*, based on South Dakota Oral History Tapes, began touring in 1990 and won the Fargo-Moorehead Community Theatre Midwestern Playwright's Merit Award in 1988. Sylvia Wheeler's poetry has often been anthologized. She has won numerous awards including the Gwendolyn Brooks Poetry Prize from the Society for the Study of Midwestern Literature, a Kansas Arts Council Award for Fiction, and a South Dakota Arts Council Individual Artist Award. Currently she is an Associate Professor of English at the University of South Dakota.

BY SYLVIA GRIFFITH WHEELER

City Limits (poems)
In the Middle: Midwestern Women Poets (anthology)
For Kids, By Kids (anthology)
This Fool History (play)
Counting Back: Voices of the Lakota and Pioneer Settlers
    (forthcoming poems, BkMk Press)

Other BkMk Offerings

In the Middle: Midwestern Women Poets, edited by Sylvia Griffith Wheeler. Poems and essays by Alberta Turner, Sonia Gernes, Diane Hueter, Janet Beeler Shaw, Patricia Hampl, Joan Yeagley, Cary Waterman, Roberta Hill Whiteman, Dorothy Selz, and Lisel Mueller.

$9.50, 120 pages, paper

A Story To Tell, poetry by Michael Paul Novak. Soundly made poems by a man firmly in the world who looks beyond surfaces and certainties. "Remarkable immediacy ... Novak brings a reader as close to the moment of experience as is possible with uncomplicated, graceful language, palpable feeling." —*Kansas City Star*.

$9.50, 72 pages, cloth with jacket

Kansas City Outloud II, poetry anthology. Edited by Dan Jaffe with an introduction by Miller Williams. Work by 32 Kansas City area poets including Stanley Banks, Sharat Chandra, Conger Beasley, Jr., George Gurley, Alfred Kisubi, David Ray, Trish Reeves, Gloria Vando and Maryfrances Wagner.

$12.95, 136 pages, cloth with jacket

Studies on Zone, poems by Alice Glarden Brand. "Moving from observations to conversations to assertions, ... reminds us that poetry is our most important communication." —*Judith Baumel*.

$8.95, 72 pages, cloth with jacket

Small Indulgences, poems by Susan Rieke. "...a quiet, firm voice. I'm impressed by both the precision of language and the precision of feeling." —*Michael Paul Novak*.

$6.50, 63 pages, paper

Kisses in the Raw Night, poems by Victoria Garton. Victoria Garton blends sensual imagery with resonant verse, magically opening the mysterious boxes of human relationships.

$8.95, 64 pages, cloth with jacket

Plumbers, poems by Robert Stewart. "These poems are moving, experienced, and, in their own hardbitten earthy way, pretty elegant. I love the way Stewart's affection for his subject, his genuine sweetness, keeps being close-shaved by a tough, realistic sense of limits. The knowledge in these poems is hard-won, the craft impressive." —*Phillip Lopate*.

$8.50, 64 pages, cloth with jacket

Seasons of the River, poems by Dan Jaffe, color photos by Bob Barrett. Prize-winning poems about the Missouri River accented with exceptional color photographs. "[These] poems are marked by strong, breathtaking beginnings and affirmative endings ... this is a book of timeless interest." —*St. Louis Post-Dispatch*.

$14.95, 64 pages, cloth (8½ x 11")

Wild Bouquet, by Harry Martinson. The first American collection of these nature poems by the Swedish Nobel Laureate. Translated and with an introduction by William Jay Smith and Leif Sjöberg.

$10.95, 76 pages, cloth with jacket

Before the Light, poems by Ken Lauter. Three narratives probe the agonies of modern life: Lauter moves from the making of a porno "snuff" film to the murder of an adult retarded son to the making of the A-bomb.

$6.95, 52 pages, cloth

The Woman in the Next Booth, poems by Jo McDougall. A native of the Arkansas Delta, Jo McDougall presents "the funk and smell of humanity," says Miller Williams. "Artful and serious work," comments Howard Nemerov.

$8.50, 64 pages, cloth with jacket

The Studs of McDonald County, poems by Joan Yeagley. "If there is a steel edge to these poems, there is a deep joy as well, something that comes when the place has been chosen and it is as rich and varied as the seasons." —*John Knoepfle*.

$6.95, 56 pages, cloth

The Eye of the Ghost: Vietnam Poems by Bill Bauer. "Bill Bauer takes us well into the experience of Vietnam with a sure sense of the catastrophe that war proved for those who were involved. These poems demonstrate not only craft and dedication to the poet's art, but also an abiding commitment to justice and compassion." — *Bruce Cutler.*

$7.95, 56 pages, cloth

The Hippopotamus: Selected Translations 1945-1985 by Charles Guenther. Poems translated from Eskimo, Greek, Hungarian, French, Italian, and Spanish. "A compact and elegant collection by an acknowledged master of the craft." — *Kansas City Star.*

$6.50, 76 pages, paper

Mbembe Milton Smith: Selected Poems. "A brooding soul with a brilliant, searching consciousness." — *Cottonwood Review.* "Mbembe was — IS — one of our most nourishing poets. He used language deftly, with lively, affectionate respect ... His legacy will continue to warm literature." — *Gwendolyn Brooks.*

$8.95, 116 pages, paper

Writing in Winter by Constance Scheerer. Includes a rewrite of the Cinderella myth and tributes to Anne Sexton and Sylvia Plath. "One of the fresher voices out of the Midwest. Her portraits of what she has seen, felt and imagined are vivid and memorable." — *David Ray.*

$5.25, 80 pages, paper

Real & False Alarms by David Allan Evans. "This book will be remembered with critical acclaim ... it deserves the widest possible readership I can encourage." — *James Cox,* editor, *Midwest Book Review.*

$5.25, 64 pages, paper

Dark Fire by Bruce Cutler. A book length narrative poem exploring the restlessness of a fading flower child. "A lively, imaginative and finely crafted tale of modern life." — *Judson Jerome, Writers Digest.*

$5.25, 64 pages, paper

Selected Poems of John Knoepfle. "Among the finest work of our time." — *Abraxas.* "Contains poems that ought to become permanent parts of the American poetic tradition." — *Chicago.*

$6.50, 110 pages, paper

The Record-Breaking Heatwave, poems by Jeff Friedman. "This is urban poetry, working class poetry, strongly felt, carefully observed, cleanly written ..." — *Donald Justice.*

$6.95, 56 pages, cloth

To Veronica's New Lover, poems by Marc Monroe Dion. "Marc Dion has a reporter's eye for the telling detail, the poet's ear for the jammed vernacular ... full of booze, bitterness, and Irish machismo in neighborhoods 'pregnant and heavy-footed with life'." — *Peg Knoepfle.*

$7.95, 64 pages, cloth

Adirondack, poems by Roger Mitchell. "Mitchell patiently stands aside, to allow these Adirondack hills, forests and people to speak for themselves.... *Adirondack* is a fine example of style, or form, growing naturally out of its own material." — *Paul Metcalf.*

$8.95, 64 pages, cloth with jacket

Mysteries in the Public Domain, poems by Walter Bargen. A Target Series Book. "...a poet of the true Heartland. His poems come from the gut by way of the heart." — *Jim Barnes.*

$6.50, 64 pages, paper

Time Winds, poems by Alfred Kisubi. Poems by a Ugandan poet reflecting the struggle for African identity under dictatorship and technology. "Clearly his poetry is in the tradition of ... distinguished voices such as those of Chinua Achebe, Wole Soyinka, Dennis Brutus and Okot P'Bitek." — *Andrew Salkey.*

$9.95, 80 pages, cloth with jacket